THREE SHEETS
IN THE WIND

By Norman Thelwell

Three Sheets in the Wind
Up the Garden Path
Compleat Tangler
Play it as it Lies

thelwell.
THREE SHEETS
IN THE WIND

Allison & Busby Limited
11 Wardour Mews
London W1F 8AN
allisonandbusby.com

First published in 1973.
This paperback edition published by Allison & Busby in 2023.

A CIP catalogue record for this book is available from
the British Library.

10 9 8 7 6 5 4 3 2 1

ISBN 978-0-7490-2927-2

Typeset in 10/15 pt Adobe Caslon Pro by
Allison & Busby Ltd.

The paper used for this Allison & Busby publication
has been produced from trees that have been legally sourced
from well-managed and credibly certified forests.

Printed and bound by
CPI Group (UK) Ltd, Croydon, CR0 4YY

CONTENTS

TECHNICAL TERMS
EXPLAINED

Guy Rope (Captain)

CROWN KNOT - - - - -

LOOK OUTS - - - - - - -

BIGHT - - - - - - - - - -

BONE IN HER TEETH - - -

SAFETY HARNESS - - - - - - - -

- - - - - ROW LOCKS

- - - - - BOOM JAWS

- - - FENDERS

MIDDLE GROUND - - - - -

- - - APPARENT WIND

DECK HANDS - - - - - -

MARINE INSURANCE - -
(FOR LETTING FLY)

COMPASS
(FOR LOSING WAY)

SHEEP SHANKS
(FOR GOING ABOUT)

LOOSE FOOTED
STANDING LUGS - - -
(FOR TRIPPING THE ANCHOR)

- - - FOOT PUMPS

HEEL

May Day (First Mate)

Entering up the log

A sailor's bunk

A sea shanty

Free board

Capsize

Personal buoyancy

Reef points

Flinder's bar

Lashing down

Losing way

Boom

A windlass

Dressed overall

Making sail

A sailing horse

Tide race

Navigation marks

By and large

Lying in the roads

The plimsoll mark

'Where's this place, mate?'

THE CALL
OF THE SEA

Sailing is the fastest growing participation sport
of modern times.

It is no longer the exclusive preserve of the very rich.

Nor does one have to be wealthy to own one's own craft.

Sailing is a family sport.

There is no room for the generation gap in a boat.

Whether your preference is for the feel of a
capricious breeze in your canvas

or for the heady excitement of a surging power boat . . .

whether you find yourself drawn irresistibly to
the open sea

or take your pleasures in inland waters –
there is nothing quite like the thrill . . .

of being in sole command of your own boat.

'I'm NOT going to be rescued by Bob and
Vera Harrington.'

SAFETY FIRST

Make sure that your vessel is seaworthy before
setting sail.

Avoid weirs.

Do nothing that may alarm or annoy bathers.

Always step right into the centre of a small boat.

Always carry enough fuel – it is difficult to obtain at sea.

And never make any signals that may be mistaken for
a distress call.

Listen carefully to weather forecasts. And above all . . .

give your friends on shore precise details of where you
intend to sail

and make sure that each member of your crew is
wearing a life jacket.

'I don't know what it means but it's a four-letter word.'

THE INTERNATIONAL
CODE OF SIGNALS

I am undergoing a speed trial.

Man overboard.

I require a tug.

Stop your vessel.
I have something important to communicate.

I am manoeuvring with difficulty.

I am in need of a pilot.

This vessel is about to depart.

Communicate with me.

Stop carrying out your intentions.

I have lost my bathing costume.

'A curse on that self-steering gear.'

RULES OF THE ROAD
FOR SAILORS

Clean off all barnacles – they will slow down your progress.

Keep well clear of rocks when leaving harbour.

Organise the dog watch.

Check your craft for stowaways.

Beware of undertow.

Be prepared for sudden squalls

and if you run into fog – give one long blast.

If you find yourself in serious trouble – have someone
ready to bail you out.

Abandon ship only as a last resort.

'If anyone hears the engine, we'll be ostracised
at the club.'

GETTING THE WIND UP:
THE BEAUFORT SCALE

FORCE 0 Do not get impatient – you could be
becalmed for weeks.

FORCE 1–2 You were warned to carry a spare
set of charts.

FORCE 3–4 You're glad she brought her mother along now.

FORCE 5–6 . . . And most of that's raw sewage.

FORCE 7–8 Your dinner WAS in the oven.

FORCE 9–10 It's going to be dicey getting her home up the A1.

FORCE **11–12** Do not worry – your house blew down
anyway.

'They'll allow me to bury you at sea but not in
these waters, I'm afraid.'

SEA FEVER

'Do you have any caviar?'

'I'm sorry mate but it's a single-handed race.'

'If you don't stop slimming, I'll have to look for fresh crew.'

'NOW can we start a family?'

'My God, Jackson! We're not going to make it.'

'You single-handed chaps are all the same.'

'Oh for pity's sake let him light it.'

'That was a near thing, Mavis.'

'I don't know why you race when you're
such a damn poor loser.'

'Remember that crump at the traffic lights?'

'What a stupid place to put an oil rig!'

'Navigation's easy – just follow the sewage back home.'

'You can always tell when it's Cowes week.'

'The daily woman's late again!'

'Who's wearing stiletto heels?'

'Hello! The cargo's shifted.'

'He hates doing the weeding.'

'They've been done! They've all been done.'

'Knee-deep in sawdust and shavings all winter – and for what?'

ALSO IN THE SERIES

BRITAIN'S BELOVED CARTOONIST

thelwell.

COMPLEAT TANGLER

Reel with laughter!

The perfect gift for any angler who appreciates the primitive thrill of hunting wild creatures, the hours spent studying minute aquatic flies, and the art of manipulating his tackle. Britain's beloved cartoonist Norman Thelwell creates reels of fun in his rip-roaring angler's guide.

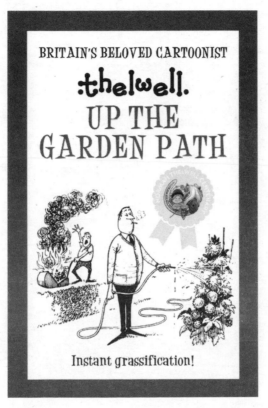

BRITAIN'S BELOVED CARTOONIST

:thelwell.
UP THE
GARDEN PATH

Instant grassification!

The perfect gift for any gardener who has experienced
overbearing neighbours, the pains of building a water feature,
unruly indoor plants; and the battle to dig the lawnmower out
from the shed. Britain's beloved cartoonist Norman Thelwell
presents a fine crop of witticisms in his hilarious gardener's
handbook.

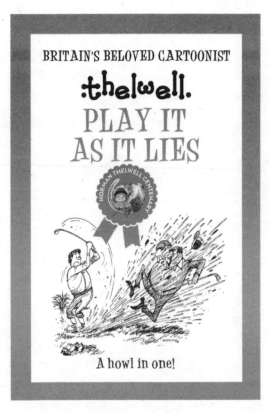

BRITAIN'S BELOVED CARTOONIST

thelwell.

PLAY IT AS IT LIES

A howl in one!

The perfect gift for any golfer who has experienced the horrors of sporting the wrong attire on course, losing his ball, or been wronged by unforgivable gamesmanship. Britain's beloved cartoonist Norman Thelwell scores a hole-in-one with his rollicking golfer's manual.

NORMAN THELWELL contributed more than 1,600 cartoons to Punch magazine, the *Sunday Express* and Tatler. Thelwell's cartoons remain a popular and wry look at British life. He was particularly well-known for his cartoons on horse riding, fishing, sailing, motoring and country pursuits and was one of the founder members of the British Cartoonists' Association.

thelwell.org.uk

To discover more great books and to
place an order visit our website at
www.allisonandbusby.com

Don't forget to sign up to our free newsletter at
www.allisonandbusby.com/newsletter
for latest releases, events and exclusive offers

Allison & Busby Books
@AllisonandBusby

You can also call us on
020 3950 7834
for orders, queries
and reading recommendations